Conquer Year 3 Science with CGP!

Ready to test the key facts in Year 3 Science? Once pupils have got to grips with all the content in our matching Year 3 Science Knowledge Organiser, they can check how much they've learned with our Knowledge Retriever!

With bonus mixed practice quizzes and a full set of answers too, this book has everything Year 3 pupils need for Science success!

CGP — still the best! ☺

Our sole aim here at CGP is to produce the highest quality books — carefully written, immaculately presented and dangerously close to being funny.

Then we work our socks off to get them out to you
— at the cheapest possible prices.

Contents

How to Use This Book 1

Plants
Plant Basics 2
The Life Cycle of Plants 4

Plants Quiz 6

Animals Including Humans
Nutrition 8
Skeletons and Muscles 10

Nutrition and The Skeleton Quiz 12

Rocks
Rocks, Fossils and Soil 14

Light
Light, Dark and Shadows 16

Forces and Magnets
Forces and Magnets 18

Rocks, Light, Forces
   & Magnets Quiz 20

Working Scientifically
Working Scientifically 22
Investigation — Growing Plants 24

Mixed Quiz 26

Answers 32

Published by CGP.

Editors: Josie Gilbert, Jake McGuffie, Luke Molloy, Rachael Rogers and George Wright

Contributors: Paddy Gannon and Tony Laukaitis

With thanks to Susan Alexander, Paul Jordin, Glenn Rogers and Charlotte Sheridan for the proofreading.

With thanks to Jan Greenway for the copyright research.

ISBN: 978 1 78908 955 4

Printed by Elanders Ltd, Newcastle upon Tyne.
Clipart from Corel®
Illustrations by: Sandy Gardner Artist, email sandy@sandygardner.co.uk

Based on the classic CGP style created by Richard Parsons.

Text, design, layout and original illustrations © Coordination Group Publications Ltd. (CGP) 2022
All rights reserved.

Photocopying this book is not permitted, even if you have a CLA licence.
Extra copies are available from CGP with next day delivery. • 0800 1712 712 • www.cgpbooks.co.uk

How to Use This Book

This book is split into different topics that you'll learn about in Year 3 Science. Every page in this book has a matching page in the Year 3 Science **Knowledge Organiser**. Before you fill in the pages in this book, you should have learnt about the topic in your lessons at school and in the Knowledge Organiser. This is what you need to do:

1 Read the pages and fill in any dotted lines as you go. One dotted line means there's one word missing — sometimes you get given the first letter of the word and sometimes you don't.

2 When you've finished, you can use the answers at the back of the book to check your work. Tick the smiley face to show how well you know the topic.

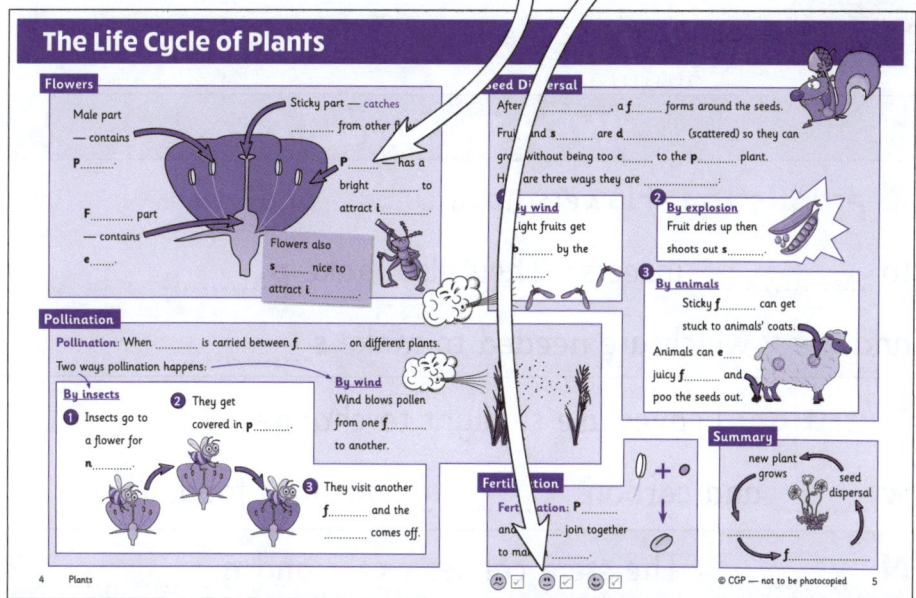

Sometimes you might have used a different word to fill in the gap from what is shown in the answers. That's okay, as long as the word has the same meaning.

There are also **Quizzes** throughout the book:
- These quizzes test content from the previous few pages, including key words. There's also a bigger 'Mixed Quiz' at the end that tests content from the whole book.
- Answers to the quizzes are at the back of the book. After you've completed a quiz, mark your answers and write your score in the box at the end of the quiz.

How to Use This Book   1

Plant Basics

Parts of a Plant

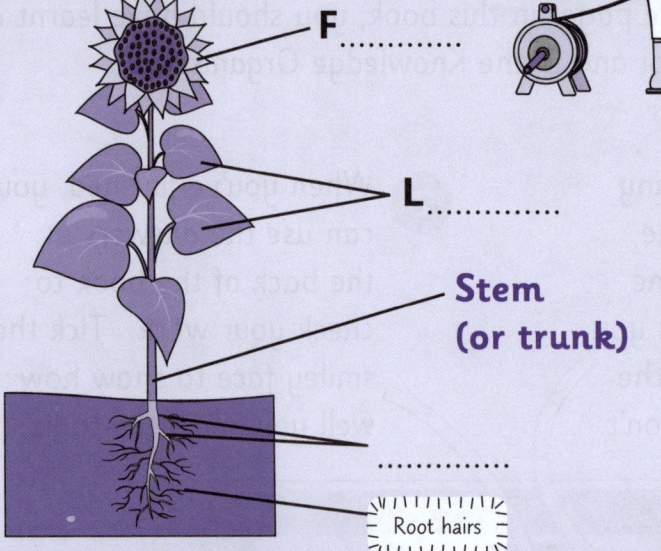

F............
L............
Stem (or trunk)
....
Root hairs

Water Transport

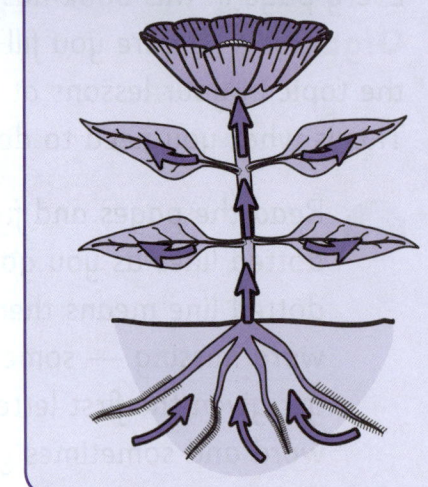

Part	What It's Needed For
Flower	**Reproduction:** Flowers have colours and smells to .... insects. They also make **p**............ and eggs, which are needed to make **s**............ .
Leaves	**Nutrition:** Leaves use sunlight to change **w**............ and carbon .... gas into food.
Stem (or trunk)	**N**................: The stem carries water and **n**................ from the **r**............ to the rest of the plant. **Support:** The stem holds the plant up towards the **l**............ .
Roots	**Nutrition:** Roots absorb **w**............ and nutrients from the soil. **S**............: Roots fix the plant to the **g**............ so it doesn't **b**........ **a**........ .

2   Plants

Water is **a**.................. from the soil by the **r**............

It is then sucked up the ....

Finally it goes into the **l**............ and flowers.

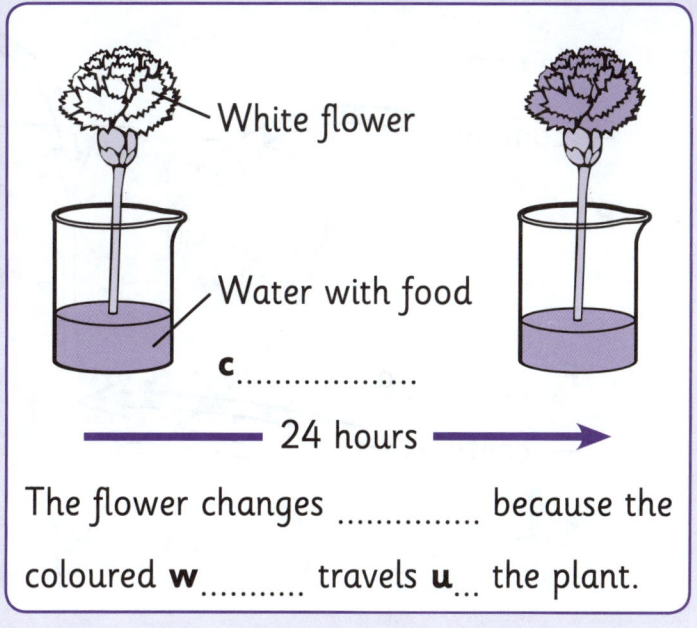

White flower

Water with food **c**..................

← 24 hours →

The flower changes .... because the coloured **w**............ travels **u**... the plant.

Five Things Plants Need

① **L**............

These are used by the leaves for nutrition.

② **Air** (which contains **c**............ ....)

③ **W**............

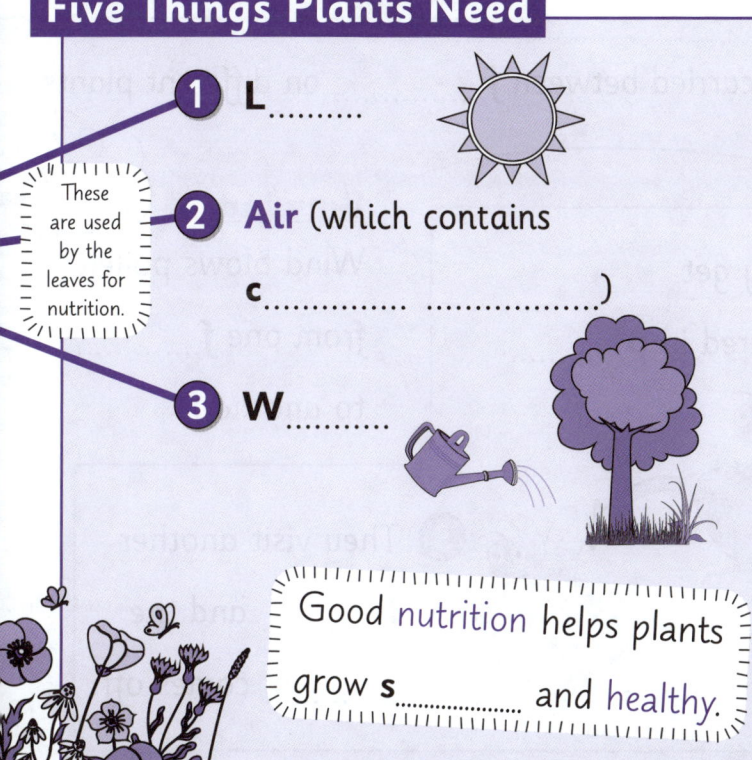

Good **nutrition** helps plants grow **s**............ and **healthy**.

④ **Nutrients** (e.g. **m**............ from soil)

⑤ **R**............ **to grow**

Different plants will need different **a**............ of these five things — e.g. ferns need lots of **w**............ but cacti only need a **l**............ **w**............

© CGP — not to be photocopied

The Life Cycle of Plants

Flowers

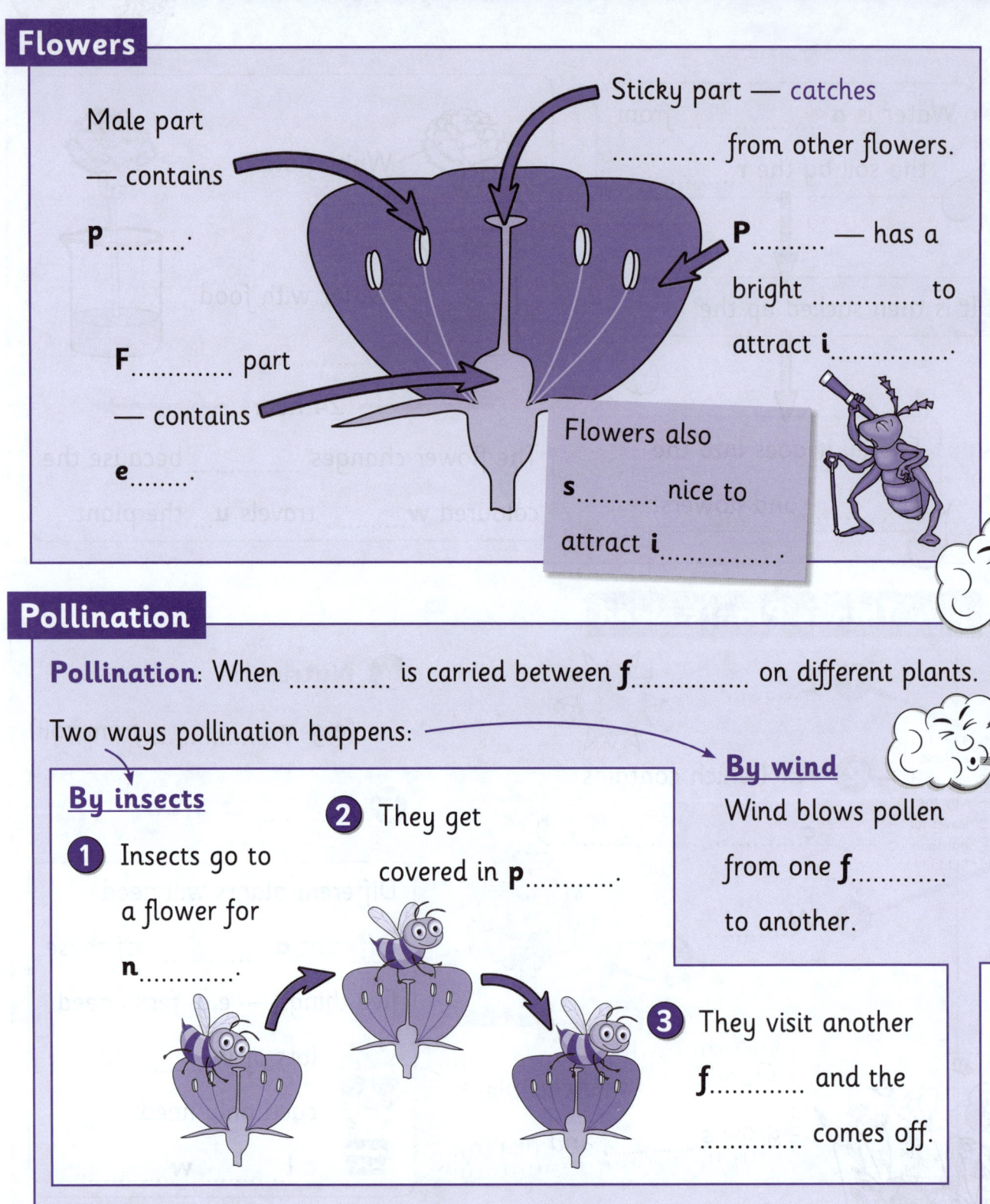

Male part — contains p............ .

F............ part — contains e........ .

Sticky part — catches .... from other flowers.

P.......... — has a bright .... to attract i............. .

Flowers also s........... nice to attract i............. .

Pollination

Pollination: When .... is carried between f............. on different plants.

Two ways pollination happens:

By insects
1. Insects go to a flower for n............. .
2. They get covered in p............. .
3. They visit another f............. and the .... comes off.

By wind
Wind blows pollen from one f............. to another.

4 Plants

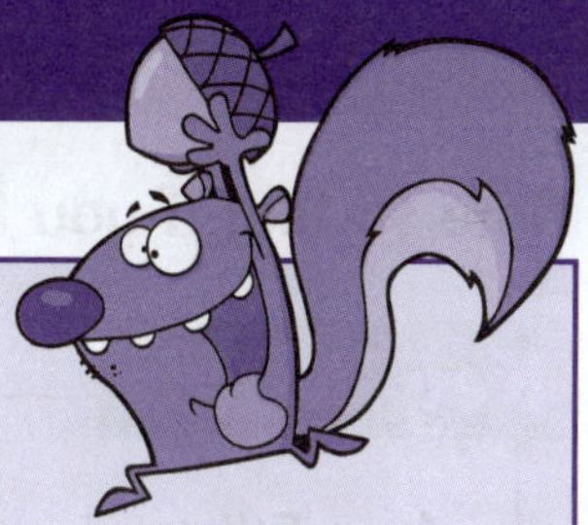

Seed Dispersal

After **f**........................, a **f**.......... forms around the seeds.

Fruits and **s**............ are **d**..................... (scattered) so they can grow without being too **c**.......... to the **p**............ plant.

Here are three ways they are ....:

1 By wind

Light fruits get **b**............ by the ....

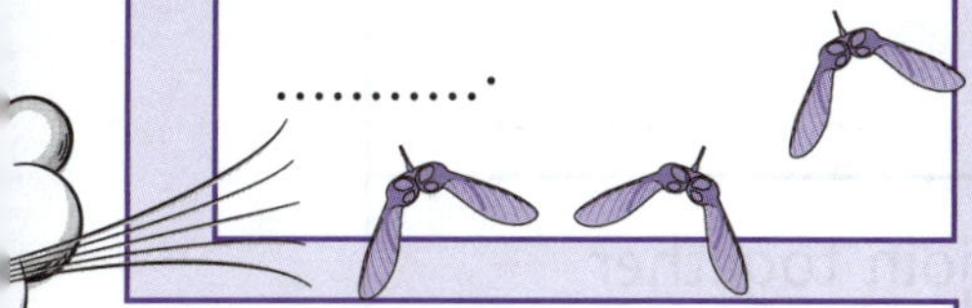

2 By explosion

Fruit dries up then shoots out **s**............ .

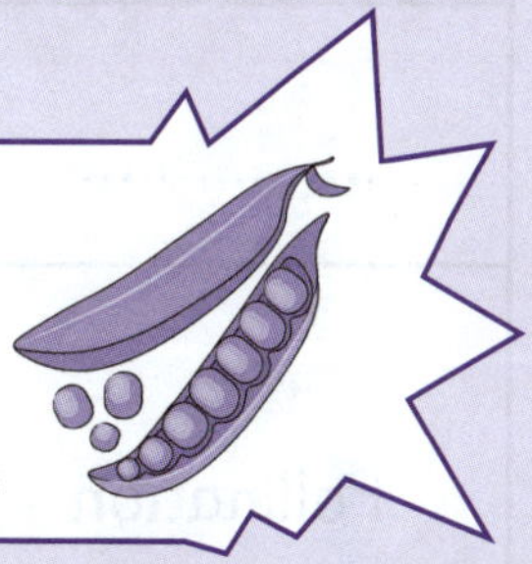

3 By animals

Sticky **f**............ can get stuck to animals' coats.

Animals can **e**...... juicy **f**............ and poo the seeds out.

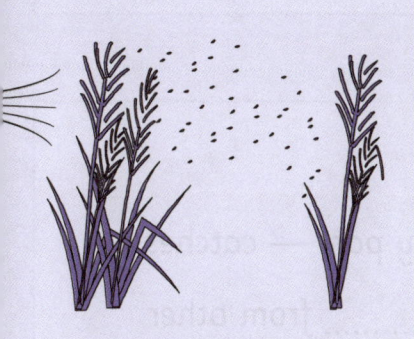

Fertilisation

Fertilisation: **P**............ and an **e**...... join together to make a ....

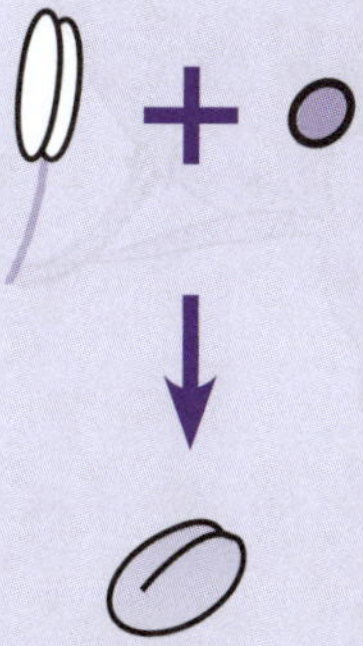

Summary

new plant grows → seed dispersal

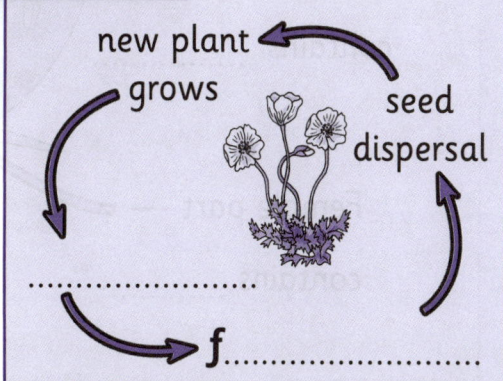

.... → **f**........................

Plants Quiz

Time to test if you know your stems from your seeds, in the first quick quiz.

Key Words

1. Fill in the gaps in this table.

Word	Definition
....	Part of a plant that uses sunlight to change water and carbon dioxide gas into food.
Pollination	....
....	When pollen and an egg join together to make a seed.

3 marks

Key Diagrams

2. Fill in the gaps in the labels for this diagram.

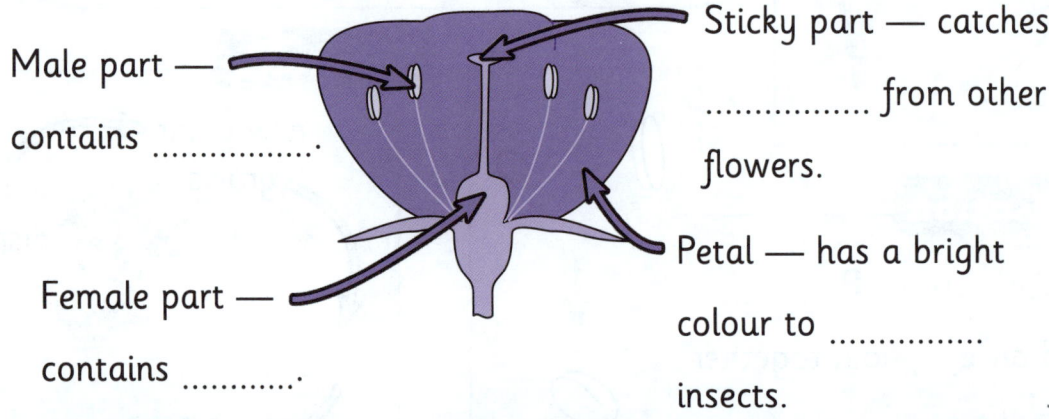

Male part — contains ....

Female part — contains ....

Sticky part — catches .... from other flowers.

Petal — has a bright colour to .... insects.

4 marks

Now Try These

3. What part of a plant absorbs water from the soil?

   ....

   1 mark

4. Write down two ways that seeds can be dispersed.

   1. .... 2. ....

   2 marks

5. Fill in the gaps below to describe how insects pollinate plants.

   Insects go to a flower for .... They get covered in pollen. They visit another .... and the pollen comes off.

   2 marks

6. What five things do plants need to grow well?

   ...., air, ..., ..., room

   3 marks

7. Maya puts a plant with a white flower in a jar of water. The water has blue food colouring.

   a) What will happen to the flower?

      It will change .... from .... to ....

   b) Why will this happen?

      Because the .... water travels .... the stem and goes into the ....

   6 marks

Score:

Nutrition

Animals and Food

Animals, including h................., can't make their own ....

Animals get n.................... from the food they eat.

A Human Diet

Humans need to eat a b................... diet to get the r........... amount of nutrients.

F.........

In m........., oils and dairy.

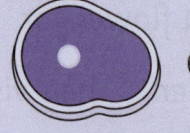 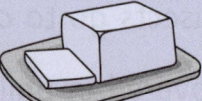

Needed for e...............

Nutrients

Proteins

In fish, meat, beans, nuts and e.........

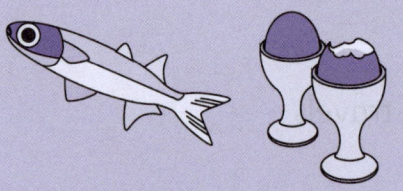

Needed for g............. and r.............

Vitamins and M...............

In f........., vegetables and dairy.

Needed to keep our cells h...............

8 Animals Including Humans

Carbohydrates — Starches and Sugars

S..................
In **b**.........., pasta and cereals.
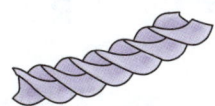

Sugars
In **b**................, cakes and sweets.

Needed for **e**................

Some **f**................ contain water too.

Water
In drinks.

Needed to **l**........

Animal Diets

Most animals eat **l**............ things to get the **n**.................... they need.

Some animals eat other ...., e.g. bears eat fish.

....
In fruit, **v**........................ and wholegrain bread.

Needed to help move food through the **g**........

Some animals eat **p**............, e.g. caterpillars eat leaves.

Skeletons and Muscles

Skeletons

A skeleton is made of **b**............ Humans have a skeleton **i**............ their body.

Collar bone

.... blade

Pelvis

T............ bone

............: Protects the brain

R......: Protect the heart and lungs

S..........: Protects the spinal cord

K...............

Different animals have **d**.................. skeletons.

Some animals don't have **s**.................., e.g. squids and snails.

Muscles

A j..........

M...............

A b..........

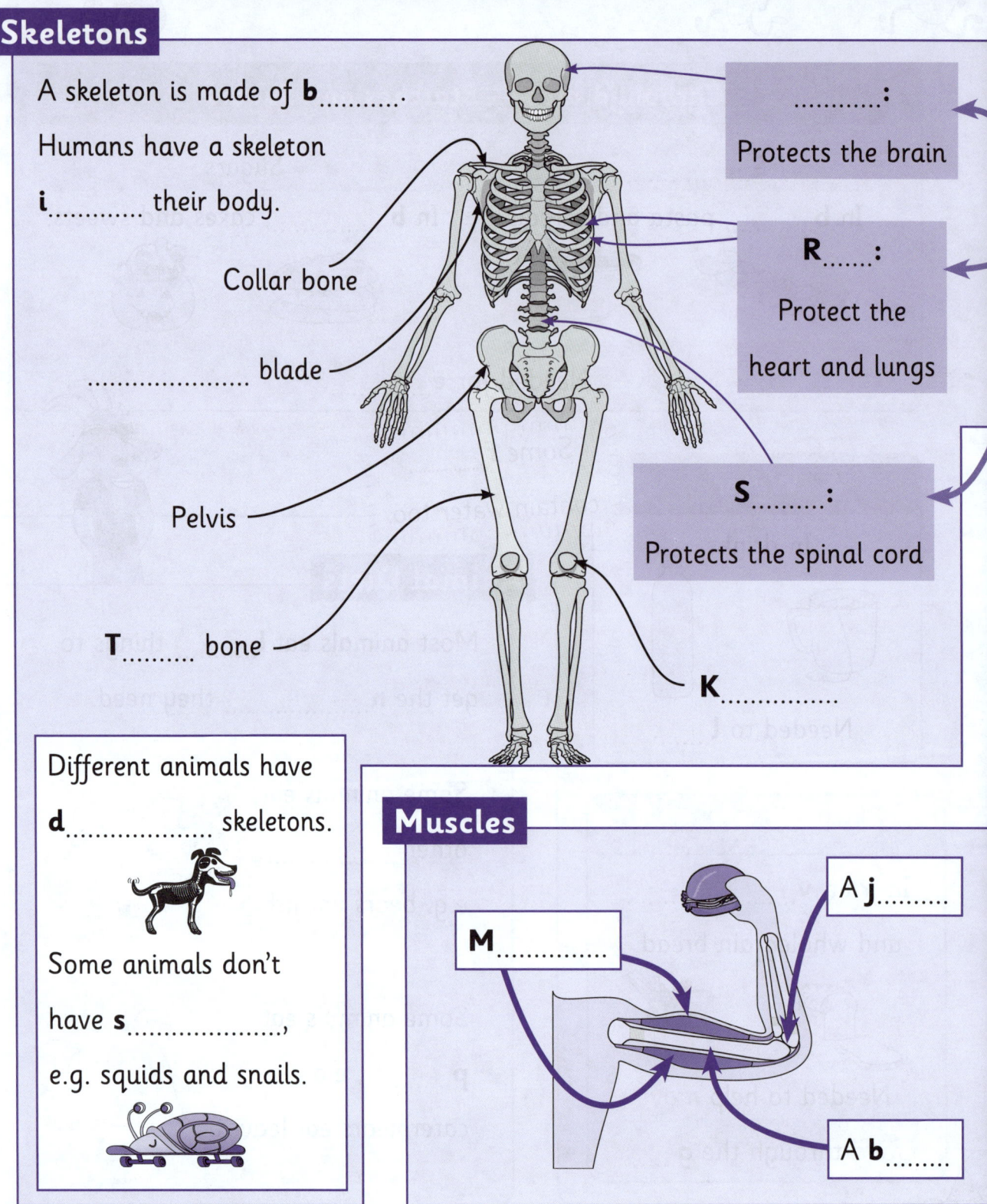

10   Animals Including Humans

A skeleton has three jobs:

1	S..............	It lets the body stand u.............. and h.......... up body parts.
2	P......................	It stops body parts getting d....................
3	Movement	Muscles are joined to the b.........., which have joints. Muscles and joints allow the skeleton to ....

Muscles work in .... to move bones — one muscle c.................... while the other r..............

.... = gets shorter.
.... = gets longer.

To pull the arm up:

This muscle c.................... and pulls on this bone.

This muscle r...............

To pull the arm down:

This muscle r...............

This muscle c.................... and pulls on this bone.

© CGP — not to be photocopied   11

Nutrition and The Skeleton Quiz

Have a crack at this quiz to see how much you know.

Key Words

1. Draw lines to match each word to its definition.

   Diet — They let the body move by pulling on bones.

   Nutrient — This protects and supports the body and allows it to move. It's made up of lots of bones.

   Muscles — A substance that a plant or animal needs to grow.

   Skeleton — The mixture of foods that a human or other animal eats.

   3 marks

Key Diagrams

2. Label this diagram of a human arm.

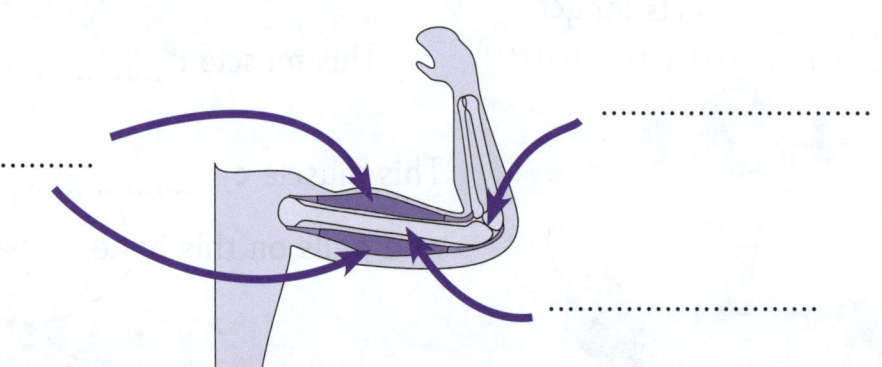

   3 marks

12 Nutrition and The Skeleton Quiz

Now Try These

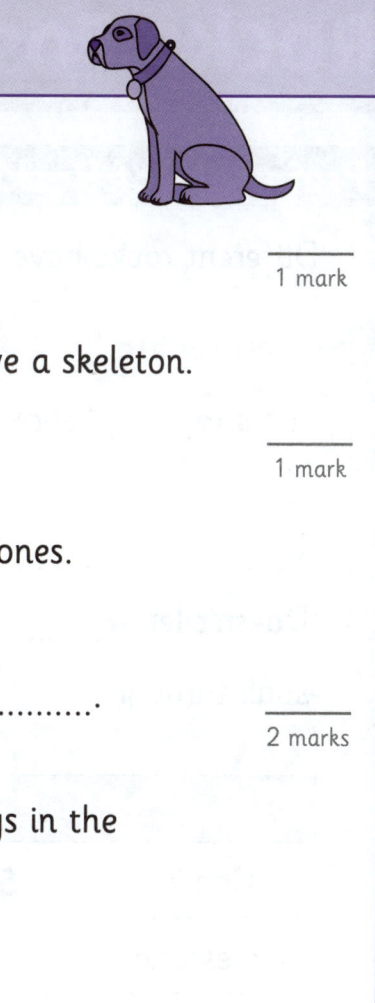

3. Where do animals get their nutrients from?

   ....

   1 mark

4. Give an example of an animal that **doesn't** have a skeleton.

   ....

   1 mark

5. Fill in the gaps to describe how muscles move bones.

   Muscles work in .... to move bones.

   One muscle contracts while the other ....

   2 marks

6. Different nutrients are needed for different things in the human body.

   a) What are proteins needed for?

   .... and ....

   b) What is fibre needed for?

   It helps move .... through the gut.

   3 marks

7. What are three jobs of a skeleton?

   1. ....

   2. ....

   3. ....

   3 marks

Score:

Rocks, Fossils and Soil

Properties of Rocks

Different rocks have different **properties**.

Permeable
Lets **w**......... soak through.

I..........................
Doesn't let **w**......... soak through.

Properties

Soft
Easy to .... or crumble.

S.............
Can hold a lot of weight.

Hard
D.............. to scratch or break down.

Hard rocks go smooth and shiny when they're polished.

Rock	Properties
Chalk	**S**........, **p**....................
Limestone	and sedimentary.
Marble	
Slate	**H**........, **i**....................
Granite	and strong.

Sedimentary rocks:
- Made from layers of **m**........ and sand.
- Can contain **f**.............

Grouping Rocks

You can **group** rocks by their **p**.................... or by the way they **l**........ . E.g. these rocks are grouped by:

C............

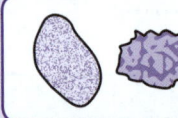
Grains

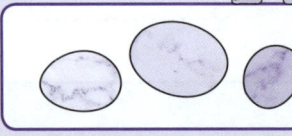
Smoothness

14   Rocks

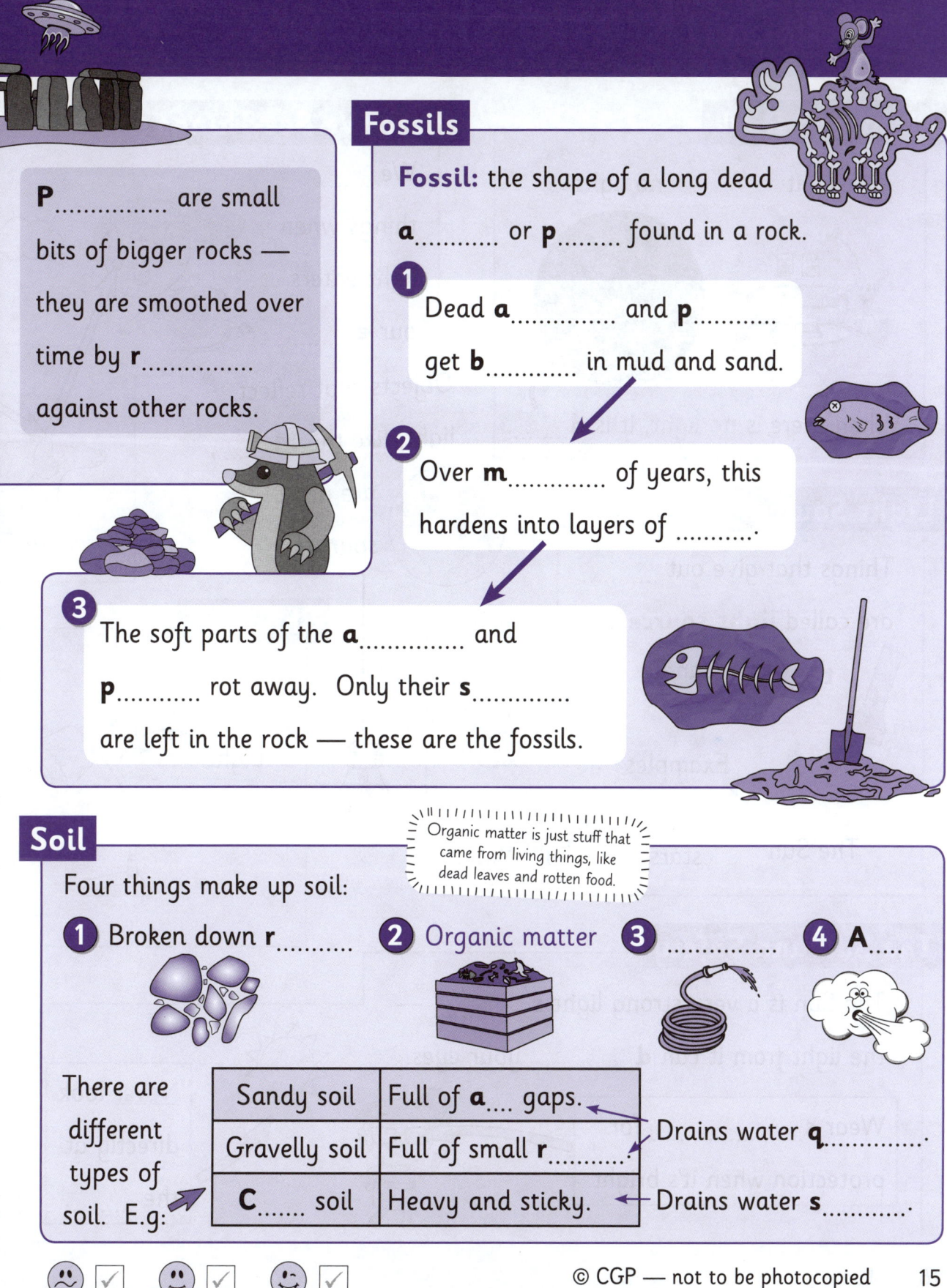

P............... are small bits of bigger rocks — they are smoothed over time by r............... against other rocks.

Fossils

Fossil: the shape of a long dead **a**............ or **p**......... found in a rock.

① Dead **a**............... and **p**............ get **b**............ in mud and sand.

② Over **m**............ of years, this hardens into layers of ....

③ The soft parts of the **a**............... and **p**............ rot away. Only their **s**............... are left in the rock — these are the fossils.

Soil

Four things make up soil:

① Broken down **r**............   ② Organic matter   ③ ....   ④ **A**......

Organic matter is just stuff that came from living things, like dead leaves and rotten food.

There are different types of soil. E.g:

Sandy soil	Full of **a**.... gaps.
Gravelly soil	Full of small **r**............
C....... soil	Heavy and sticky.

Drains water **q**...............
Drains water **s**...............

© CGP — not to be photocopied   15

Light, Dark and Shadows

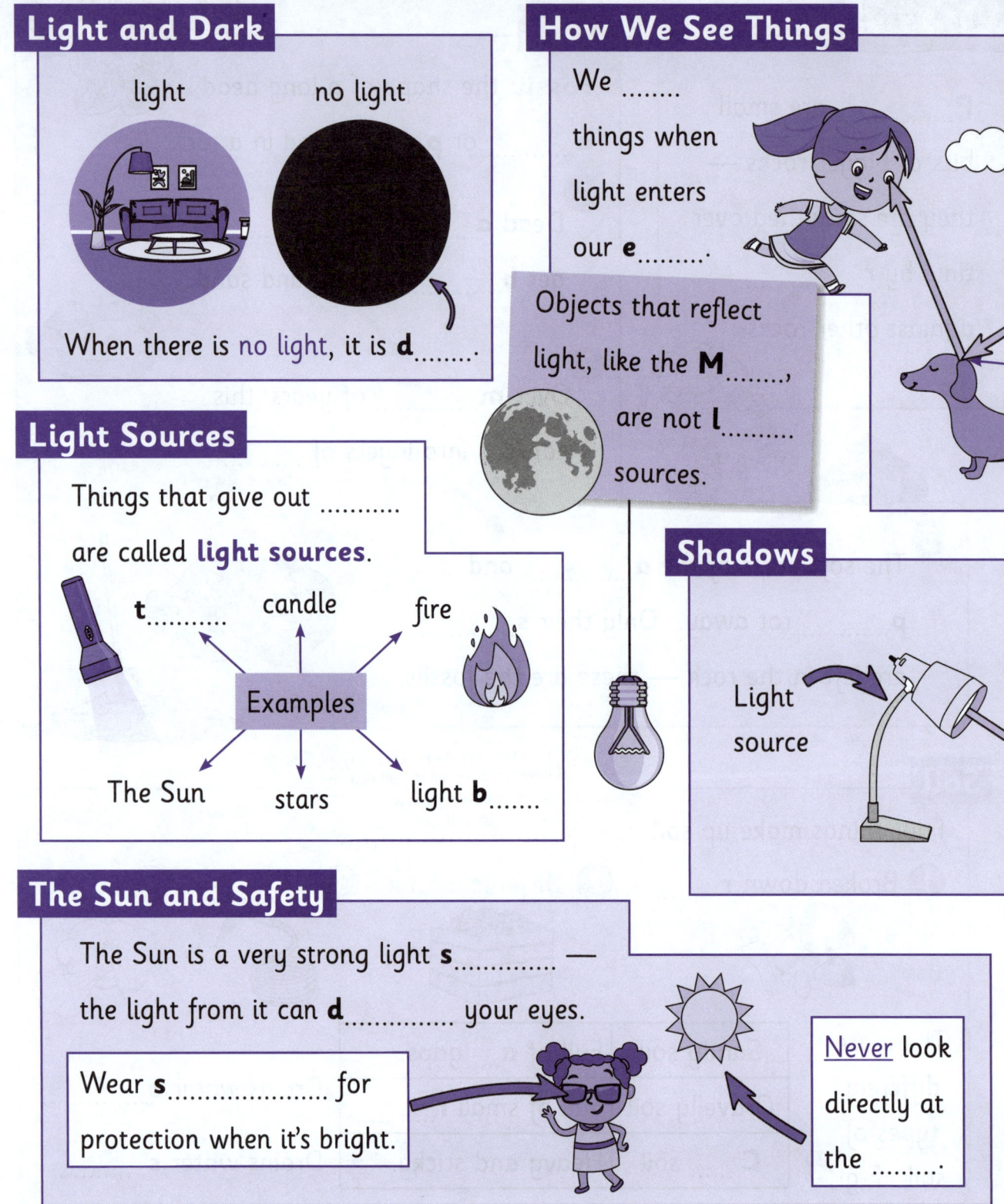

Reflection

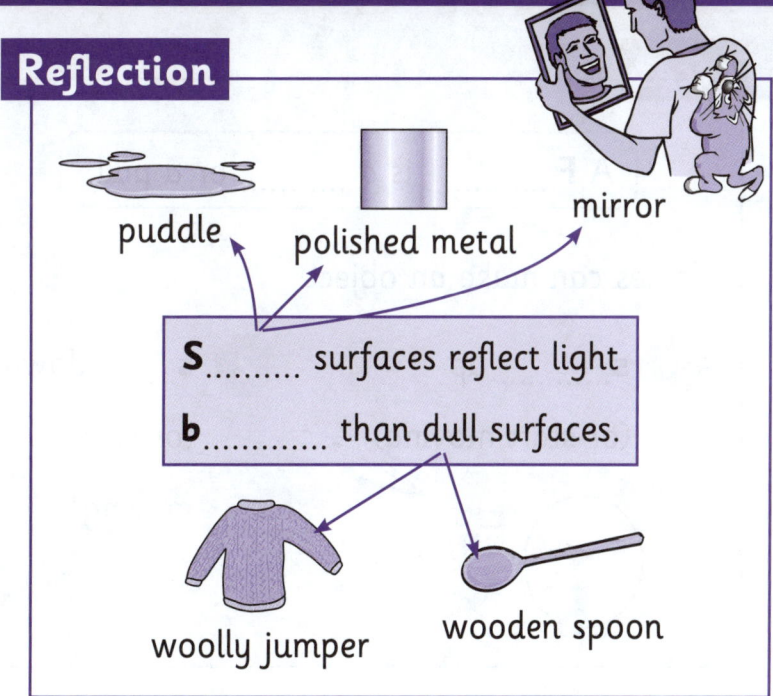

S.......... surfaces reflect light b............ than dull surfaces.

puddle, polished metal, mirror, woolly jumper, wooden spoon

Light r................. off objects.

O............... object blocks light. S............... is formed.

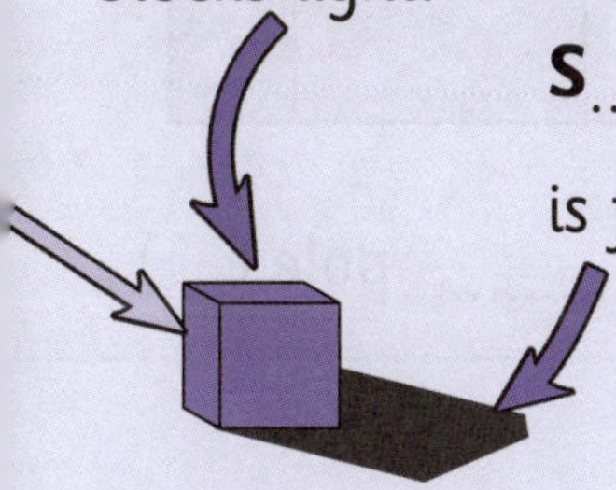

1 The m.......... directly overhead a light source is, the shorter the shadow.

2 The c............ a light source is to an o............, the larger the shadow.

Forces and Magnets

Forces

A **F**............ is a .... or a pull.

Forces can make an object:

1 **s**............ up (or start moving)

2 **s**........ down (or stop moving)

3 change **d**..................

Forces and Contact

Some forces need two objects to **t**............

M.............. forces don't need objects to **t**............

Magnetic Poles

N............ pole (N)

.... pole (....)

Magnetic Materials

Some materials are **m**.............., e.g. iron and **s**............

Other materials are not ...., e.g. brass, aluminium and **w**............

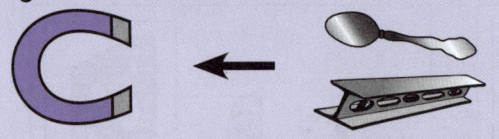
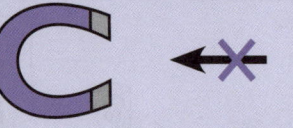

Magnetic materials are **a**.................. to either **p**........ of a magnet.

18   Forces and Magnets

Movement on Surfaces

R............ **surfaces**

(e.g. roads)

s......... down moving objects quickly.

Cars can stop **q**.................... on roads.

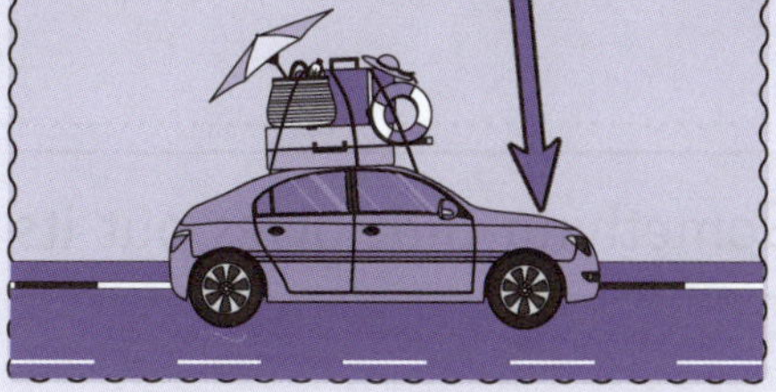

S............... **surfaces**

(e.g. ice)

don't **s**......... down moving objects much.

Skates move **f**.......... on ice.

4 change **s**............

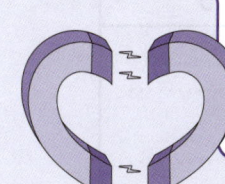

Opposite poles **a**................

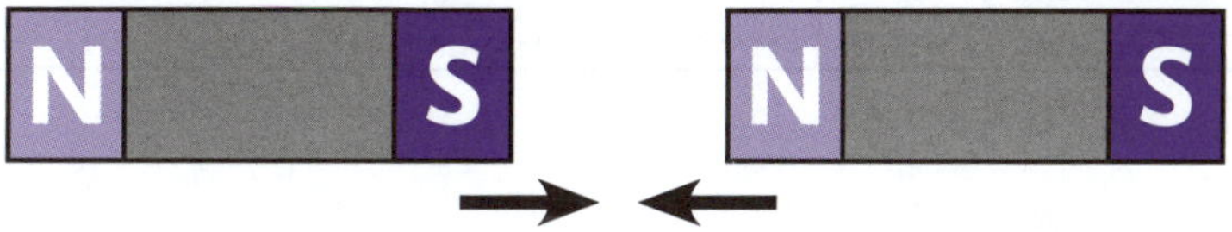

Magnets move **t**................ each other.

Like poles **r**............

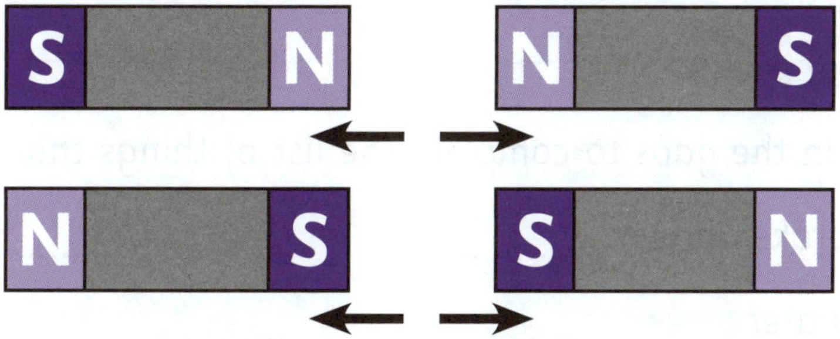

Magnets move **a**.......... from each other.

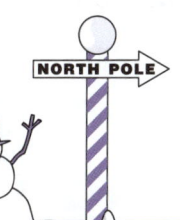

19

Rocks, Light, Forces & Magnets Quiz

Time for another quiz — this one covers a variety of things from p.14-19.

Key Words

1. Fill in the gaps in this table.

Word	Definition
....	A push or a pull.
....	The shape of a long dead animal or plant found in a rock.
Magnetic	....
....	Something that gives out its own light.
Impermeable	....

5 marks

Now Try These

2. Fill in the gaps to complete the list of things that make up soil.

   - broken down ....
   - .... matter
   - water
   - ....

3 marks

3. Complete these sentences about magnets.

   Magnets don't need to .... for there to be a magnetic force between them. Magnets have .... poles — a North pole and a South pole. The force between two .... poles (e.g. two North poles) will cause two magnets to move .... from each other.

   4 marks

4. Describe how an object's shadow changes if it moves closer to a light source.

   ....

   1 mark

5. Give two examples of rocks that are soft and permeable.

   1. ....   2. ....

   2 marks

6. Write down whether each of these sentences is true or false.

   a) A dull surface will reflect light better than a shiny surface. ....

   b) A soft rock is easier to scratch or crumble than a hard rock. ....

   c) A moving object will slow down quicker on a rough surface than on a smooth surface. ....

   3 marks

Score:

© CGP — not to be photocopied

Working Scientifically

Planning an Experiment

Three steps for planning an experiment:

1. Write down the .... you want to answer.

2. Write a **m**.............. — this is what you're going to do.

   Include: 1. what you will measure or observe,

   2. what **e**.................. you will use.

   The experiment must be a .... TEST — a test where you only change one thing and keep **e**.................. else the same.

3. Write a .... — this is what you think will happen.

Getting Results

R.............. can be observations or measurements.

Observations — these are what you can **s**........

Describe observations clearly.

You can see if your conclusion matches your prediction.

Conclusions

Experiments end with a **c**.................. — a sentence that sums up your **f**...............

The sentence is usually written like: ➡ 'As one thing **c**.............. like this, another thing **c**.............. like this.'

E.g. 'the later the time in the afternoon, the .... the post's shadow'.

Look for patterns in your **r**.............. to help you draw **c**..................

22   Working Scientifically

Measurements — these are what you can ....

When making measurements, use sensible e...................... with a sensible s..............

E.g. to measure lengths, it's best to use a ruler that's longer than the length you need to measure (but not way too long).

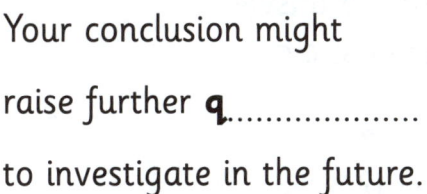

Your conclusion might raise further q..................... to investigate in the future.

E.g. 'how does the length of the post's shadow change in the morning?'

Recording Results in Tables

Time of day	Length of post's shadow (cm)
12 pm	5
1.30 pm	15
3 pm	30
4.30 pm	50

M.............................. are recorded in each r..........

Each c.............. has a heading including the u..............

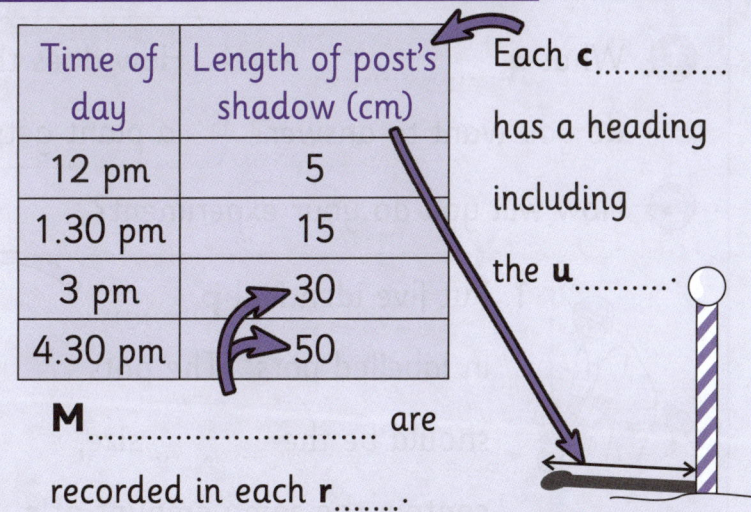

Displaying Results in Bar Charts

Length of the post's shadow at different times ← Title

...-axis

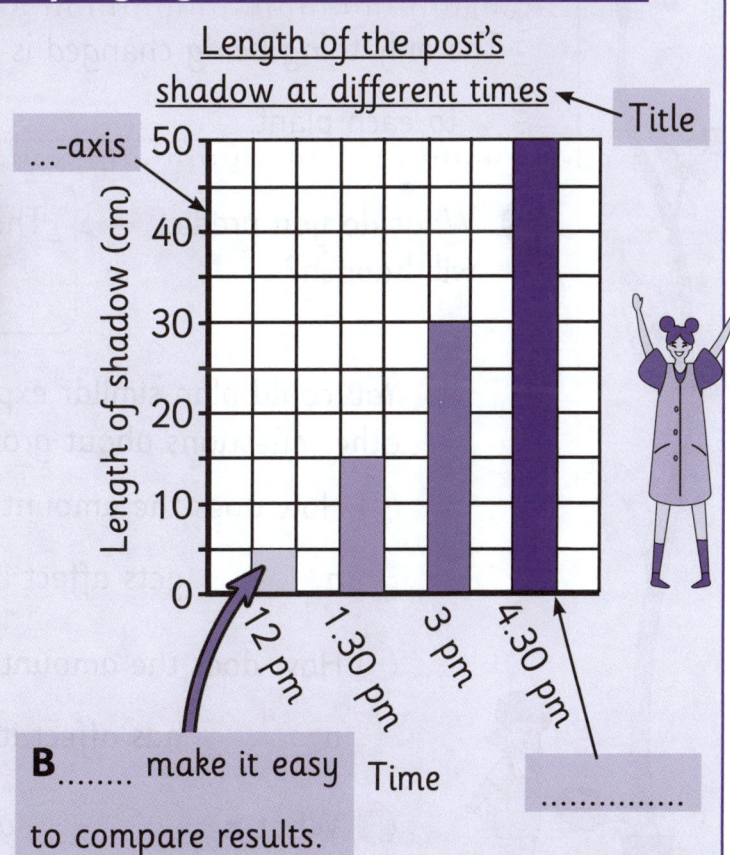

Time

B.......... make it easy to compare results.

© CGP — not to be photocopied   23

Investigation – Growing Plants

Planning your Experiment

1 What **q**.................... do you want to answer? → How does the amount of water a plant gets affect its growth?

2 How will you do your experiment?

1. Put five identical **p**............ in labelled pots. The pots should be the .... size, contain the same amount of **s**...... and be put in the same **p**............

The only thing being changed is the amount of **w**................ given to each plant. .... else must stay the same.

3 What do you predict will happen? → The .... water a plant gets, the **t**............ it will grow.

You could plan similar experiments to answer other questions about growing plants, e.g.:

🍃 How does the amount of **l**............ a .... gets affect its growth?

🍃 How does the amount of space a .... has affect its growth?

🍃 What **n**.................... are best for plant growth?

24 Working Scientifically

2. Use a **m**.............. cylinder to measure out a different amount of **w**............ for each plant. Water the plants with this amount each day.

3. After a week, measure the **h**.............. of each plant with a **r**............. Record your measurements in a table.

Results

Plant	Amount of water given per day (ml)	Height of plant after a week (cm)
A	0	0 (plant died)
B	10	4
C	20	8
D	30	10
E	40	0 (plant died)

Conclusion

The results show that the more **w**............ a plant gets, the **m**........ it grows — as long as it doesn't get .... much water.

The thing you .... goes on the y-axis.

Height of plants given different amounts of water after a week

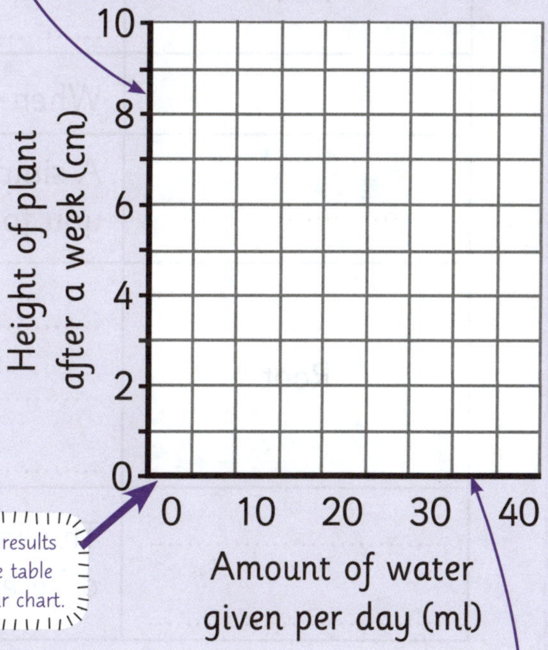

Plot the results from the table on the bar chart.

The thing you .... goes on the x-axis.

© CGP — not to be photocopied   25

Mixed Quiz

It's the quiz to end all quizzes — time to strut your stuff.

Key Words

1. Fill the gaps in the table below.

Word	Definition
....	A type of rock made from layers of sand or mud. They can contain fossils.
(Magnetic) Pole	....
Opaque	....
....	When two magnets push apart.
....	A simple sentence that sums up what you found out in an experiment.
Root	....
....	This means eating the right mix of different nutrients to keep you healthy.

7 marks

2. Draw lines to match each word to its definition.

Organic matter — The part of a plant needed for reproduction.

Prediction — A plant or animal getting the nutrients it needs to stay healthy.

Flower — Anything that came from living things.

Nutrition — What you think will happen in an experiment.

3 marks

3. Use the words in the box to complete the definitions below.

attract   experiment   petal
permeable   fair test   water

a) ....: the colourful part of the flower that helps .... insects.

b) ....: a material which allows .... to soak through it.

c) ....: an .... where only one thing is changed, and everything else is kept the same.

6 marks

© CGP — not to be photocopied   27

Key Diagrams

4. Label the bones on the human skeleton below.

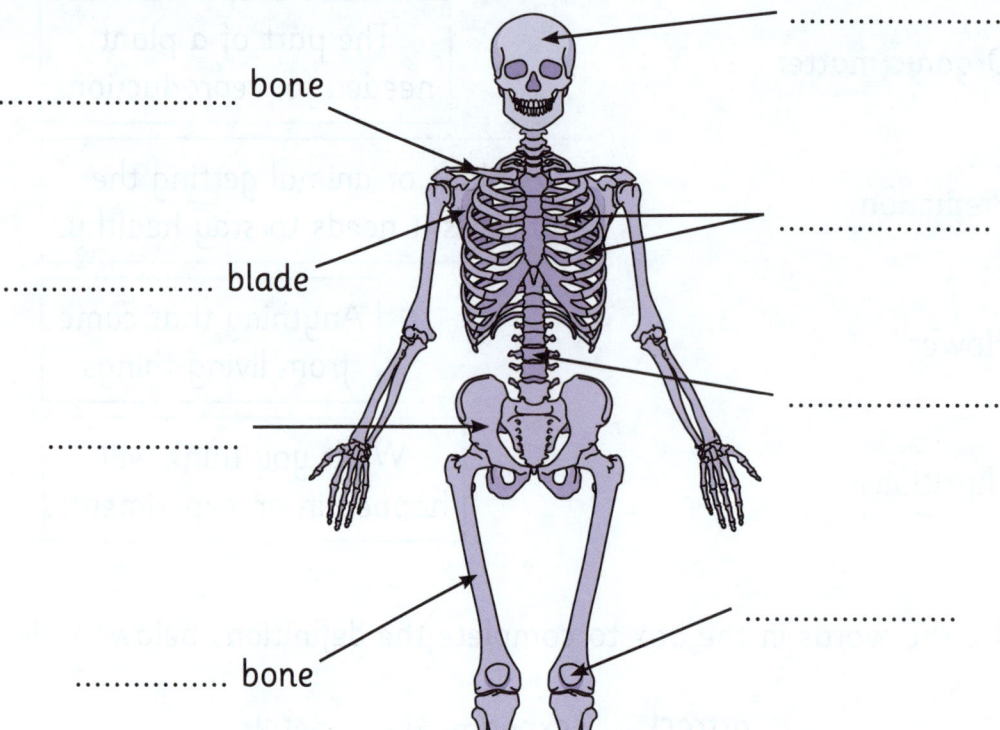

.... bone

.... blade

.... bone

....

....

....

....

.... bone

8 marks

5. Fill in the missing poles on the bar magnets below.
   The arrows show the direction the magnets move in.

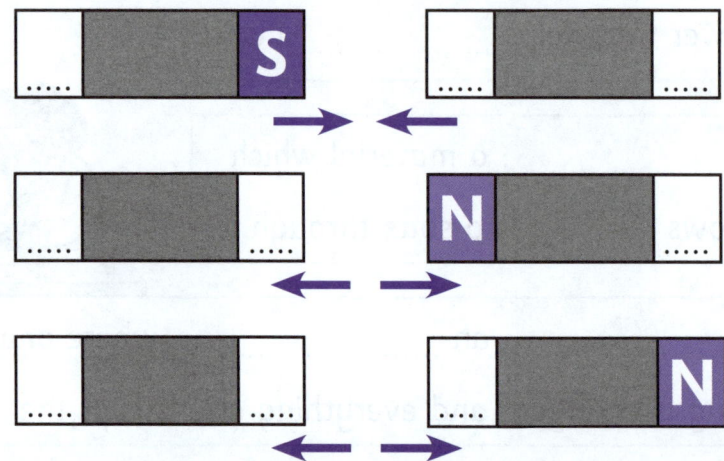

3 marks

28   Mixed Quiz

Now Try These

6. Which one of these three types of soil drains water **slowly**: sandy, gravelly or clay?

   ....

   1 mark

7. What are two things you can do to protect your eyes from being damaged by sunlight?

   1. ....

   2. ....

   2 marks

8. Write down the two ways by which pollination can happen.

   1. .... 2. ....

   2 marks

9. Complete the list of nutrients needed in a balanced diet.

   1. Carbohydrates   4. ....

   2. Fibre   5. ....

   3. Vitamins and .... 6. ....

   4 marks

10. The skeleton is needed for protection of body parts. Which body part (or parts) do the following bones protect?

    a) Spine   ....

    b) Skull   ....

    c) Ribs   ....

    3 marks

11. Describe two things that the stem of a plant is needed for.

   1. ....

   ....

   2. ....

   ....

   2 marks

12. Write down whether each of these sentences is true or false.

   a) Things that give out light
   are called light sources.   ....

   b) Shadows are longer when a
   light source is directly overhead.   ....

   c) Light is reflected from surfaces.   ....

   3 marks

13. Fill in the gaps to describe how fossils are formed.

   Dead animals and plants get .... in mud and sand.

   Over millions of years, this hardens into .... of rock.

   The soft parts of the animals and plants .... away.

   Only their .... are left in the rock —

   these are the fossils.

   4 marks

14. Where should you write the units in a results table?

   ....

   1 mark

30   Mixed Quiz

15. Some materials are magnetic, but others aren't magnetic.

    a) What does it mean if a material is magnetic?

    ....

    b) Give two materials that **are** magnetic and two that **aren't**.

    magnetic: .... and ....

    not magnetic: .... and ....

    5 marks

16. Explain why seed dispersal is important for plants.

    ....

    ....

    1 mark

17. What does it mean if a rock is soft?

    ....

    1 mark

18. Describe how the skeleton supports the body.

    ....

    ....

    1 mark

19. Explain why leaves are important for a plant. Use the words sunlight, carbon dioxide and water in your answer.

    ....

    ....

    1 mark

Score:

Answers

Pages 2-3 — Plant Basics

Parts of a Plant

Diagram: **Flower**
Leaves
Stem (or trunk)
Roots

Table:

Flower	Reproduction: Flowers have colours and smells to **attract** insects. They also make **pollen** and eggs, which are needed to make **seeds**.
Leaves	Nutrition: Leaves use sunlight to change **water** and carbon **dioxide** gas into food.
Stem (or trunk)	**Nutrition**: The stem carries water and **nutrients** from the **roots** to the rest of the plant. Support: The stem holds the plant up towards the **light**.
Roots	Nutrition: Roots absorb **water** and nutrients from the soil. Support: Roots fix the plant to the **ground** so it doesn't **blow away**.

Water Transport

Water is **absorbed** from the soil by the **roots**.
It is then sucked up the **stem**.
Finally it goes into the **leaves** and flowers.
Water with food **colouring**.
The flower changes **colour** because the coloured **water** travels **up** the plant.

Five Things Plants Need

1. **Light**
2. Air (which contains **carbon dioxide**)
3. **Water**
4. Nutrients (e.g. **minerals** from soil)
5. **Room** to grow

Good nutrition helps plants grow **strong** and healthy.

Different plants will need different **amounts** of these five things — e.g. ferns need lots of **water** but cacti only need a **little water**.

Pages 4-5 — The Life Cycle of Plants

Flowers

Male part — contains **pollen**.
Female part — contains **eggs**.
Sticky part — catches **pollen** from other flowers.
Petal — has a bright **colour** to attract **insects**.
Flowers also **smell** nice to attract **insects**.

Pollination

Pollination: When **pollen** is carried between **flowers** on different plants.

By insects:
1. Insects go to a flower for **nectar**.
2. They get covered in **pollen**.
3. They visit another **flower** and the **pollen** comes off.

By wind: Wind blows pollen from one **flower** to another.

Fertilisation

Fertilisation: **Pollen** and an **egg** join together to make a **seed**.

Seed Dispersal

After **fertilisation**, a **fruit** forms around the seeds.

Fruits and **seeds** are **dispersed** (scattered) so they can grow without being too **close** to the **parent** plant.

Here are three ways they are **dispersed**:

1. By wind
   Light fruits get **blown** by the **wind**.
2. By explosion
   Fruit dries up then shoots out **seeds**.
3. By animals
   Sticky **fruits** can get stuck to animals' coats.
   Animals can **eat** juicy **fruits** and poo the seeds out.

Answers

Summary

new plant grows → **pollination** → **fertilisation** → seed dispersal

Pages 6-7 — Plants Quiz

Key Words

1. **Leaf** — Part of a plant that uses sunlight to change water and carbon dioxide gas into food.
   Pollination — **When pollen is carried from the flower of one plant to the flower of another**.
   Fertilisation — **When pollen and an egg join together to make a seed**.
   (3 marks)

Key Diagrams

2. Male part — contains **pollen**
   Female part — contains **eggs**
   Sticky part — catches **pollen** from other flowers
   Petal — has a bright colour to **attract** insects
   (4 marks)

Now Try These

3. **Roots** (1 mark)
4. Any two from e.g.:
   By wind
   By explosion
   By animals
   (2 marks)
5. Insects go to a flower for **nectar**.
   They get covered in pollen. They visit another **flower** and the pollen comes off.
   (2 marks)
6. **light**, air, **water**, **nutrients**, room (3 marks)
7. a) It will change **colour** from **white** to **blue**.
   b) Because the **coloured** water travels **up** the stem and goes into the **flower**.
   (6 marks)

Pages 8-9 — Nutrition

Animals and Food

Animals, including **humans**, can't make their own **food**.
Animals get **nutrients** from the food they eat.

A Human Diet

Humans need to eat a **balanced** diet to get the **right** amount of nutrients.

Fats
In **meat**, oils and dairy.
Needed for **energy**.

Proteins
In fish, meat, beans, nuts and **eggs**.
Needed for **growth** and **repair**.

Vitamins and **Minerals**
In **fruit**, vegetables and dairy.
Needed to keep our cells **healthy**

Carbohydrates — Starches and Sugars
Starches
In **bread**, pasta and cereals.
Sugars
In **biscuits**, cakes and sweets.
Needed for **energy**.

Water
In drinks.
Needed to **live**.
Some **foods** contain water too.

Fibre
In fruit, **vegetables** and wholegrain bread.
Needed to help move food through the **gut**.

Animal Diets

Most animals eat **living** things to get the **nutrients** they need.
Some animals eat other **animals**, e.g. bears eat fish.
Some animals eat **plants**, e.g. caterpillars eat leaves.

Answers 33

Answers

Pages 10-11 — Skeletons and Muscles

Skeletons

A skeleton is made of **bones**. Humans have a skeleton **inside** their body.

Diagram:
Collar bone
Shoulder blade
Pelvis
Thigh bone
Skull: Protects the brain
Ribs: Protect the heart and lungs
Spine: Protects the spinal cord
Kneecap

Different animals have **different** skeletons.
Some animals don't have **skeletons**, e.g. squids and snails.

Table:

1. **Support**	It lets the body stand **upright** and **holds** up body parts.
2. **Protection**	It stops body parts getting **damaged**.
3. Movement	Muscles are joined to the **bones**, which have joints. Muscles and joints allow the skeleton to **move**.

Muscles

Diagram:
Muscles
A **joint**
A **bone**

Muscles work in **pairs** to move bones — one muscle **contracts** while the other **relaxes**.

Contracts = gets shorter.
Relaxes = gets longer.

To pull the arm up: This muscle **contracts** and pulls on this bone. This muscle **relaxes**.
To pull the arm down: This muscle **relaxes**. This muscle **contracts** and pulls on this bone.

Pages 12-13 — Nutrition and The Skeleton Quiz

Key Words

1. Diet — **The mixture of foods that a human or other animal eats.**
   Nutrient — **A substance that a plant or animal needs to grow.**
   Muscles — **They let the body move by pulling on bones.**
   Skeleton — **This protects and supports the body and allows it to move. It's made up of lots of bones.** (3 marks for all lines drawn correctly, otherwise 2 marks for at least two lines drawn correctly or 1 mark for one line drawn correctly)

Key Diagrams

2.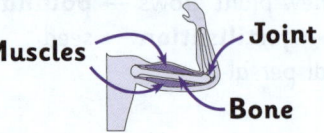

(3 marks)

Now Try These

3. **food** (1 mark)
4. e.g. **a squid / a snail** (1 mark)
5. Muscles work in **pairs** to move bones. One muscle contracts while the other **relaxes**. (2 marks)
6. a) **Growth** and **repair**
   b) It helps move **food** through the gut. (3 marks)
7. **Support Protection Movement** (3 marks)

Pages 14-15 — Rocks, Fossils and Soil

Properties of Rocks

Permeable
Lets **water** soak through.

Impermeable
Doesn't let **water** soak through.

Soft
Easy to **scratch** or crumble.

Hard
Difficult to scratch or break down.

Strong
Can hold a lot of weight.

34   Answers

Answers

Table: **Soft**, **permeable** and sedimentary.
Hard, **impermeable** and strong.

Sedimentary rocks:
- Made from layers of **mud** and sand.
- Can contain **fossils**.

Pebbles are small bits of bigger rocks — they are smoothed over time by **rubbing** against other rocks.

Grouping Rocks

You can group rocks by their **properties** or by the way they **look**.

E.g. these rocks are grouped by: **Colour**, Grains, Smoothness

Fossils

Fossil: the shape of a long dead **animal** or **plant** found in a rock.

1. Dead **animals** and **plants** get **buried** in mud and sand.
2. Over **millions** of years, this hardens into layers of **rock**.
3. The soft parts of the **animals** and **plants** rot away. Only their **shapes** are left in the rock — these are the fossils.

Soil

Four things make up soil:
1. Broken down **rocks**
2. Organic matter
3. **Water**
4. **Air**

Sandy soil — Full of **air** gaps.
Gravelly soil — Full of small **rocks**.
Drains water **quickly**.
Clay soil — Heavy and sticky. Drains water **slowly**.

Pages 16-17 — Light, Dark and Shadows

Light and Dark

When there is no light, it is **dark**.

How We See Things

We **see** things when light enters our **eyes**.
Light r**eflects** off objects.
Objects that reflect light, like the **Moon**, are not **light** sources.

Reflection

Shiny surfaces reflect light **better** than dull surfaces.

Light Sources

Things that give out **light** are called light sources.

Examples: **torch**, candle, fire, The Sun, stars, light **bulb**

The Sun and Safety

The Sun is a very strong light **source** — the light from it can **damage** your eyes.

Wear **sunglasses** for protection when it's bright.
Never look directly at the **Sun**.

Shadows

Diagram: Light source
Opaque object blocks light.
Shadow is formed.

1. The **more** directly overhead a light source is, the shorter the shadow.
2. The **closer** a light source is to an **object**, the larger the shadow.

Pages 18-19 — Forces and Magnets

Forces

A **Force** is a **push** or a pull.

Forces can make an object:
1. **speed** up (or start moving)
2. **slow** down (or stop moving)
3. change **direction**
4. change **shape**

Answers 35

Answers

Movement on Surfaces

Rough surfaces (e.g. roads) **slow** down moving objects quickly.

Cars can stop **quickly** on roads.

Smooth surfaces (e.g. ice) don't **slow** down moving objects much.

Skates move **fast** on ice.

Forces and Contact

Some forces need two objects to **touch**.

Magnetic forces don't need objects to **touch**.

Magnetic Poles

North pole (**N**)

South pole (**S**)

Opposite poles **attract**. Magnets move **towards** each other.

Like poles **repel**. Magnets move **away** from each other.

Magnetic Materials

Some materials are **magnetic**, e.g. iron and **steel**.

Other materials are not **magnetic**, e.g. brass, aluminium and **wood**.

Magnetic materials are **attracted** to either **pole** of a magnet.

Pages 20-21 — Rocks, Light, Forces & Magnets Quiz

Key Words

1. **Force** — A push or a pull.
   Fossil — The shape of a long dead animal or plant found in a rock.
   Magnetic — **A material that's attracted to a magnet.**
   Light source — Something that gives out its own light.
   Impermeable — **A material which doesn't allow water to soak through it.**
   (5 marks)

Now Try These

2. broken down **rocks**, **organic** matter, water, **air**
   (3 marks)

3. Magnets don't need to **touch** for there to be a magnetic force between them. Magnets have **two** poles — a North pole and a South pole. The force between two **like** poles (e.g. two North poles) will cause two magnets to move **away** from each other.
   (4 marks)

4. The shadow gets bigger.
   (1 mark)

5. e.g. **chalk**, **limestone**
   (2 marks)

6. a) False
   b) True
   c) True (3 marks)

Pages 22-23 — Working Scientifically

Planning an Experiment

1. Write down the **question** you want to answer.

2. Write a **method** — this is what you're going to do.
   Include: 1. what you will measure or observe,
   2. what **equipment** you will use.

   The experiment must be a **FAIR** TEST — a test where you only change one thing and keep **everything** else the same.

3. Write a **prediction** — this is what you think will happen.

Getting Results

Results can be observations or measurements.

Observations — these are what you can **see**.

Measurements — these are what you can **measure**.

When making measurements, use sensible **equipment** with a sensible **scale**.

Recording Results in Tables

Each **column** has a heading including the **units**.

Measurements are recorded in each **row**.

36 Answers

Answers

Displaying Results in Bar Charts

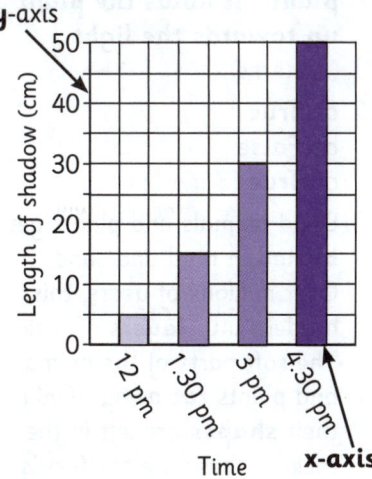

Bars make it easy to compare results.

Conclusions

Experiments end with a **conclusion** — a sentence that sums up your **findings**.

The sentence is usually written like:
'As one thing **changes** like this, another thing **changes** like this.'
E.g. 'the later the time in the afternoon, the **longer** the post's shadow.'

Look for patterns in your **results** to help you draw **conclusions**.

Your conclusion might raise further **questions** to investigate in the future.

Pages 24-25 — Investigation — Growing Plants

Planning your Experiment

What **question** do you want to answer?

How will you do your experiment?
1. Put five identical **plants** in labelled pots. The pots should be the **same** size, contain the same amount of **soil** and be put in the same **place**. The only thing being changed is the amount of **water** given to each plant. **Everything** else must stay the same.
2. Use a **measuring** cylinder to measure out a different amount of **water** for each plant. Water the plants with this amount each day.
3. After a week, measure the **height** of each plant with a **ruler**. Record your measurements in a table.

What do you predict will happen?
The **more** water a plant gets, the **taller** it will grow.

You could plan similar experiments to answer other questions about growing plants, e.g.:
How does the amount of **light** a **plant** gets affect its growth?
How does the amount of space a **plant** has affect its growth?
What **nutrients** are best for plant growth?

Results

The thing you **measure** goes on the y-axis.

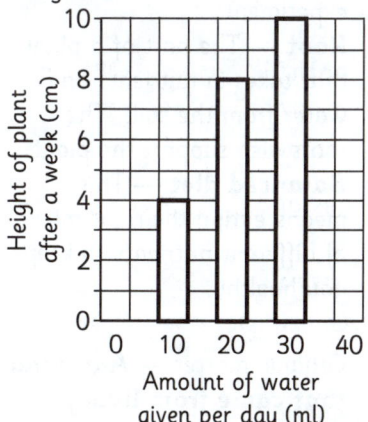

The thing you **change** goes on the x-axis.

Conclusion

The results show that the more **water** a plant gets, the **more** it grows — as long as it doesn't get **too** much water.

Pages 26-31 — Mixed Quiz

Key Words

1. **Sedimentary rock** — A type of rock made from layers of sand or mud. They can contain fossils.
   (Magnetic) Pole — **The end of a magnet. A magnet has a North and a South pole**.
   Opaque — **A material that doesn't let light through it**.
   Repel — When two magnets push apart.

Answers   37

Answers

Conclusion — A simple sentence that sums up what you found out in an experiment.
Root — The part of a plant that takes in nutrients and water from the soil. The roots also support the plant.
Balanced diet — This means eating the right mix of different nutrients to keep you healthy.
(7 marks)

2. Organic matter — **Anything that came from living things.**
Prediction — **What you think will happen in an experiment.**
Flower — **The part of a plant needed for reproduction.**
Nutrition — **A plant or animal getting the nutrients it needs to stay healthy.**
(3 marks for all lines drawn correctly, otherwise 2 marks for at least two lines drawn correctly or 1 mark for one line drawn correctly)

3. a) **Petal**: the colourful part of the flower that helps **attract** insects. (2 marks)
   b) **Permeable**: a material which allows **water** to soak through it. (2 marks)
   c) **Fair test**: an **experiment** where only one thing is changed, and everything else is kept the same. (2 marks)

Key Diagrams
4.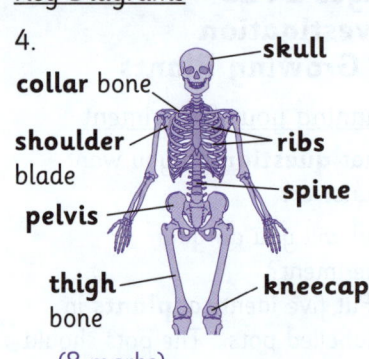
(8 marks)

5.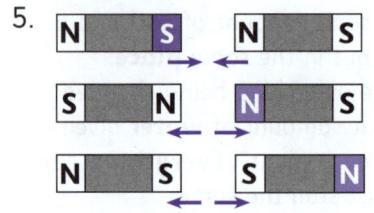
(1 mark for each correct pair of magnets)

Now Try These
6. **Clay** (1 mark)
7. **Wear sunglasses when it's bright. Never look directly at the Sun.** (2 marks)
8. **by insects, by wind** (2 marks)
9. Carbohydrates, Fibre, Vitamins and **minerals**, Fats, Water, Protein (4 marks)
10. a) **The spinal cord**
    b) **The brain**
    c) **The heart and lungs**
    (3 marks)

11. **It carries water and nutrients to the rest of the plant. It holds the plant up towards the light.** (2 marks)
12. a) **True**
    b) **False**
    c) **True** (3 marks)
13. Dead animals and plants get **buried** in mud and sand. Over millions of years, this hardens into **layers** of rock. The soft parts of the animals and plants **rot** away. Only their **shapes** are left in the rock — these are the fossils. (4 marks)
14. **In the column heading.** (1 mark)
15. a) **It is attracted to a magnet.** (1 mark)
    b) Magnetic: e.g. **iron** and **steel**
    Not magnetic: any two from, e.g. **brass / aluminium / wood** (4 marks)
16. **So new plants can grow without being too close to the parent plant.** (1 mark)
17. **It's easy to scratch or crumble.** (1 mark)
18. **It lets the body stand upright and holds up body parts.** (1 mark)
19. **They use sunlight to turn water and carbon dioxide (gas) into food for the plant.** (1 mark)

38   Answers